The California Gold Rush

BY
CINDY BARDEN

COPYRIGHT © 2001 Mark Twain Media, Inc.

ISBN 1-58037-179-5

Printing No. CD-1525

Mark Twain Media, Inc., Publishers
Distributed by Carson-Dellosa Publishing Company, Inc.

Table of Contents

About the American History Series

Welcome to *The California Gold Rush,* one of 12 books in the Mark Twain Media, Inc., American History series for students in grades four to seven.

The activity books in this series are designed as stand-alone material for classrooms and home-schoolers or as supplemental material to enhance your history curriculum. Students can be encouraged to use the books as independent study units to improve their understanding of historical events and people.

Each book provides challenging activities that enable students to explore history, geography, and social studies topics. The activities provide research opportunities and promote critical reading, thinking, and writing skills. As students learn about the people and events involved in the Gold Rush era, they will draw conclusions; write opinions; compare and contrast historical events, people, and places; analyze cause and effect; and improve mapping skills. Students will also have the opportunity to apply what they learn to their own lives through reflection, creative writing, and hands-on activities.

Students can further increase their knowledge and understanding of historical events by using reference sources at the library and on the Internet. Students may need assistance to learn how to use search engines and discover appropriate web sites.

Titles of books for additional reading appropriate to the subject matter at this grade level are included in each book.

Although many of the questions are open-ended, an answer key is included at the back of the book for questions with specific answers.

Share a journey through history with your students as you explore the books in the Mark Twain Media, Inc., American History series:

Discovering and Exploring the Americas
Life in the Colonies
The American Revolution
The Lewis and Clark Expedition
The Westward Movement
The California Gold Rush
The Oregon and Sante Fe Trails
Slavery in the United States
The Civil War
Abraham Lincoln and His Times
The Reconstruction Era
Industrialization in America

Time Line of *The California Gold Rush*

1828   Gold was discovered at Dahlonega, Georgia.

1834   John Sutter emigrated to the United States.

1842   Don Francisco Lopez discovered gold in the roots of an onion at Placeritas Canyon in the San Fernando Valley.

1846 -
1848   The Mexican War was fought between the United States and Mexico.

1847   Yerba Buena was renamed the Town of San Francisco.

1848   **January:** James Marshall discovered gold while building a lumber mill for John Sutter.
February: The United States gained Arizona, California, Nevada, New Mexico, Utah, and western Colorado from Mexico after the Mexican War.
March: The *California Star* reported the non-native population of San Francisco was 575 males, 177 females, and 60 children.
March: Gold was discovered by Mormons on the south fork of the American River.
March: The *Californian* printed the first story of the gold discovery.
July 18: Word of the gold strike reached Los Angeles.
September: Gold dust was worth $16 an ounce.
November: Zachary Taylor was elected president.

1849   **February:** The first ship carrying prospectors arrived in California.
April: Wagon trains with 20,000 people were headed for the Gold Rush.
December: By end of this year, 80,000 had arrived in California in search of gold. Army records show that 716 enlisted men deserted between July 1, 1848, and December 31, 1849.
December: The population of San Francisco was estimated at 15,000.

1850   **July:** President Taylor died; Millard Fillmore became president.
September: California became a state.

1852   Franklin Pierce was elected president.

1853   The Gadsden Purchase was made for $10 million.

1854   The world's largest gold nugget was discovered—162 pounds.

Time Line of *The California Gold Rush*

1856   The first American camel expedition set out from Texas.
James Buchanan was elected president.

1858   The discovery of gold in Colorado began another gold rush.

1859   Oregon became a state.

1860   First Pony Express rider left St. Joseph, Missouri.
Abraham Lincoln was elected president.

1861   The Civil War began.
Transcontinental telegraph service began.

1864   President Lincoln was reelected.

1865   President Lincoln was assassinated; Andrew Johnson became president.

1867   Alaska was purchased from Russia for $7.2 million in gold.

1868   Ulysses S. Grant was elected president.

1869   The Transcontinental Railroad was completed.
Major John Powell began the exploration of the Colorado River.

1872   Yellowstone became the first national park.
President Grant was reelected.

1875   Gold was discovered in South Dakota.

1877   Black Bart held up his first stagecoach.
Silver was discovered at Tombstone, Arizona.
Deposits of gold, silver, and lead were discovered in Leadville, Colorado.

1878   The Silver Rush began in Colorado.

1896   Gold was discovered in Alaska.
Another Gold Rush began in Colorado.
The Klondike Gold Rush began.

Name: _____ Date: _____

Gold Fever Infects Thousands

Gold Fever infected tens of thousands of people in North and South America, Europe, and Asia. It affected people of every age, social class, and occupation—farmers, merchants, doctors, lawyers, rich men, and poor ones. Everyone with gold fever had one common goal—to cure the fever by searching for gold in California.

The fever began with the discovery of gold by James Marshall in January 1848 at the site where a mill was being built on land owned by John Sutter. He reportedly stated, "Hey boys, … I believe I've found a gold mine!"

As soon as this news spread, people swarmed to northern California using every means of transportation available. Fortune seekers walked, rode horses or mules, traveled in wagons and stagecoaches, or sailed thousands of miles in search of a dream.

What happened to John Sutter and James Marshall, the one who owned the land and the one who found the gold that began the mad rush to California? Did they cure the fever? Did thousands of miners become rich beyond their wildest dreams?

For most, that dream turned into a nightmare of hardship, disease, poverty, and sometimes death. For every prospector who found enough gold to become wealthy, thousands more lost everything they had and left the gold fields poorer than when they arrived.

Most who traveled to California in search of gold never intended to stay. They planned to make their fortunes, return home, and continue with their normal lives, but it rarely happened that way. Whether they found gold or not, stayed or returned home, everyone who traveled to California found that life was never the same again.

1. Why do you think people called it "gold fever"? _____

   _____

   _____

2. How was gold fever like a disease? _____

   _____

   _____

Name: _____ Date: _____

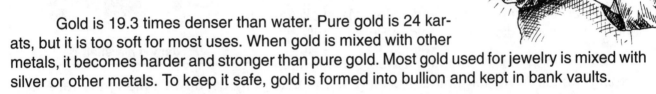

What Is Gold?

Gold is a rare soft metal found in nature. Only five-billionths of Earth's crust is gold.

Gold has been prized for thousands of years. Because it is soft, it is easier to work with than other metals. When heated to 1,943°F, gold melts and becomes liquid. Melted gold can be poured into various shapes. Gold can be hammered into sheets thinner than most paper or made into a fine thread.

In nature, gold is usually found mixed with other minerals. Any combination of minerals that includes some gold is called gold ore. Small flakes of gold are easier to find than gold nuggets. Most nuggets are small, but one found in Australia weighed 152 pounds!

Gold is 19.3 times denser than water. Pure gold is 24 karats, but it is too soft for most uses. When gold is mixed with other metals, it becomes harder and stronger than pure gold. Most gold used for jewelry is mixed with silver or other metals. To keep it safe, gold is formed into bullion and kept in bank vaults.

1. Write five-billionths as a decimal. _____

Use reference sources.

2. What is the chemical symbol for gold? _____

3. Why are these two letters used? _____

_____

Use a dictionary to define these words.

4. alloy _____

_____

5. nugget _____

_____

6. density _____

_____

7. karat (carat) _____

_____

8. bullion _____

_____

Name: _____ Date: _____

Gold Discovered at Sutter's Mill

James Marshall, construction supervisor of a saw-mill being built for John Sutter, was trying to solve problems that prevented the water from flowing forcefully enough to keep the waterwheel turning properly. He had workers deepening and widening the waterway. Each morning he checked the work and the flow of the water.

On the morning of January 24, 1848, Marshall was checking the progress of the work when he noticed a few glittering flakes of gold. Returning quickly to the mill, Marshall shouted to the men, "Boys, … I believe I have found a gold mine!"

In an interview some years later, Marshall described the day he discovered gold at Sutter's mill.

James Marshall

"One morning in January, it was a clear, cold morning; I shall never forget that morning. I was taking my usual walk along the race after shutting off the water, my eye was caught with the glimpse of something shining in the bottom of the ditch. There was about a foot of water running then. I reached my hand down and picked it up; it made my heart thump, for I was certain it was gold." … James W. Marshall

After collecting more samples over the next few days, Marshall hurried to Sacramento to tell John Sutter the big news.

1. If you discovered gold in your backyard, who would you tell first? Why?

_____

_____

_____

2. If you discovered a million dollars in gold, how would it change your life?

_____

_____

_____

3. What would be the first thing you would buy with the money? Why?

_____

_____

4. On your own paper, list three advantages and three disadvantages of having a million dollars.

Name: _____ Date: _____

Meet John Sutter

When John Sutter arrived in California in 1839, that area was still part of Mexico. He convinced the Mexican government to give him 50,000 acres of land in the Sacramento Valley. After the Mexican War ended in 1848, California became part of the United States.

Sutter built a fort of adobe bricks near where the American and Sacramento Rivers joined. In time, he owned thousands of cattle, horses, sheep, and pigs; he controlled ranches, a gristmill, a tannery, and a hat factory. He also had a bakery and blanket factory, as well as spinning, weaving, blacksmith, carpentry, and shoemaking businesses.

John Sutter's road to California was a long one. In 1834 he left his home in Switzerland to escape his business debts and emigrated to America. He traveled to Fort Vancouver in the Oregon Territory, visited Alaska, and sailed to the Hawaiian Islands before settling in California.

When James Marshall brought him proof of the discovery of gold, Sutter asked Marshall to keep his discovery a secret. Marshall agreed. The workers also promised to keep the discovery secret until the mill was finished.

A secret is difficult to keep, however, especially one as exciting as the discovery of gold. Even Sutter himself could not keep quiet. Within days of the discovery, he wrote in a letter: "I have made a discovery of a gold mine which, according to the experiments we have made, is extremely rich."

1. Why do you think John Sutter wanted to keep the discovery of gold on his property a secret?

   _____

   _____

   _____

2. What do you think this saying means? "The only way two people can keep a secret is if one of them is dead."

   _____

   _____

   _____

3. Do you agree or disagree? Why? _____

   _____

   _____

Name: _____ Date: _____

The Secret Leaks Out

A few days after Sutter learned about the gold, Jacob Wittmer, a teamster employed by Sutter, received some gold when he delivered supplies to the mill. When he returned to the fort, he used the gold to buy brandy. Soon everyone at the fort knew.

Sutter's secret made it to San Francisco as early as March 15, 1848. The news appeared as a small notice on the last page of the *Californian*.

> GOLD MINE FOUND: "In the newly made raceway of the Saw Mill recently erected by Captain Sutter, on the American Fork, gold has been found in considerable quantities. One person brought thirty dollars worth to New Helvetia, gathered there in a short time. California, no doubt, is rich in mineral wealth, great chances here for scientific capitalists. Gold has been found in almost every part of the country."

1. This announcement didn't have much effect on the people of San Francisco. Why do you think there was so little reaction to the article?

   _____

   _____

   _____

In May 1848, Sam Brannan, a Mormon elder, visited Sutter's Mill. Excited about finding gold, he returned to San Francisco. Waving a bottle of gold dust, he shouted "Gold! Gold! Gold from the American River!" The news was like lighting a stick of dynamite; everyone exploded.

Gold fever struck immediately after Sam Brannan made his announcement. Within days the city was nearly empty. The *Californian* suspended publication on May 29 with these words.

"The majority of our subscribers and many of our advertisers have closed their doors and places of business and left town ... The whole country, from San Francisco to Los Angeles and from the seashore to the Sierra Nevada, resounds with the sordid cry of gold! GOLD!! Gold, while the field is left half-planted, the house half-built, and everything neglected but the manufacture of shovels and pickaxes."

2. Use a dictionary to define *sordid*. _____

   _____

3. How do you think the writer of this editorial felt about everyone leaving to search for gold?

   _____

   _____

   _____

Name: _____ Date: _____

The Rush Begins

The news of gold spread by ship to Hawaii and Oregon. By mid-summer, settlers in Oregon were pulling up stakes and heading south to join the Gold Rush.

In July, the army sent Colonel Richard Mason to check out the rumors and write a report. He found thousands of miners panning for gold in the American River. Mason estimated that about 4,000 miners were finding a total of $30,000 to $50,000 per day in gold.

Mason's report had an immediate effect on soldiers stationed at Los Angeles. Army records show that 716 enlisted men deserted between July 1, 1848, and December 31, 1849.

"Laboring men at the mines can now earn in one day more than double a soldier's pay and allowances for a month," Mason stated in his report.

On August 8, 1848, a St. Louis newspaper reported that gold was being "collected at random and without any trouble" on the American River. Other major newspapers printed similar reports.

President Polk confirmed the discovery of gold in a message to Congress on December 5. "The accounts of the abundance of gold in that territory are of such an extraordinary character as would scarcely command belief were they not corroborated by the authentic reports of officers in the public service ..."

Newspapers printed the President's words along with exaggerated reports of how easy it was to find gold nuggets. The following was reported on December 6, 1848, by the *Hartford Daily Courant:*

"The California gold fever is approaching its crisis ... By a sudden and accidental discovery, the ground is represented to be one vast gold mine. Gold is picked up in pure lumps, twenty-four carats fine. Soldiers are deserting their ranks, sailors their ships, and everybody their employment, to speed to the region of the gold mines."

1. If 4,000 miners found $40,000 worth of gold a day, how much did each miner find on the average? _____

2. At that rate, what would have been the yearly earning if a miner worked 365 days?

_____

3. How would you have felt about going to California if you had read the newspaper reports? Would you have been tempted? Why or why not?

_____

_____

_____

Name: _____ Date: _____

The Forty-Niners

News of gold found at Sutter's Mill and other places in California caused one of the largest and wildest migrations in history. Between 75,000 and 100,000 people made their way to the California gold fields in 1849.

Nicknamed "forty-niners," most of the gold seekers were men. By 1850, women accounted for only eight percent of the population of California.

Those who rushed to the gold fields of California were also called the "Argonauts of '49." The term Argonauts referred to people from Greek mythology who sailed on the ship *Argo.*

1. James Marshall discovered gold at Sutter's Mill in January 1848. Why did it take until 1849 for most of the miners to get to California?

   _____

   _____

   _____

   _____

   _____

2. Use reference sources to find the name of the leader of the mythical Argonauts and what they were searching for.

   _____

   _____

   _____

   _____

   _____

3. Read about the adventures of the Argonauts. Why do you think those who went to California in search of gold were called argonauts?

   _____

   _____

   _____

   _____

   _____

4. On your own paper, draw a cartoon showing the forty-niners heading for California.

Name: _____ Date: _____

California, Here I Come

Most trails to the West began at Independence or St. Joseph, Missouri, or Council Bluffs, Iowa. There was never one single trail to California but rather several major routes with variations. The Oregon Trail, Santa Fe Trail, and California Trail were the three most commonly used.

Those traveling with wagon trains had to take routes that were not the most direct because of several natural obstacles: the canyons of Colorado, the Sierra Nevada Mountains, and the deserts around the Great Salt Lake.

In April 1849, 20,000 people set out in wagon trains for the gold fields of California. Thousands more followed in the next few years. Many were men who rode horses or mules. Some walked most of the way.

1. Use reference sources to learn more about one of the major routes to California. List obstacles and hardships travelers faced.

_____

_____

_____

_____

_____

_____

_____

_____

2. Use reference sources. Make a copy of a U.S. roadmap. Trace the Oregon, Santa Fe, or California Trail in black. In another color, trace the roads people can take today from the same starting point to the same destination.

3. Select one of the phrases listed below or one of your own. On your own paper, explain how it might apply to the hazards of traveling to the gold fields in the 1850s.

"When the going gets tough, the tough get going."
"It's a jungle out there."
"A journey of a thousand miles must begin with a single step."

Name: _____ Date: _____

Bumpy Roads and Sleepless Nights

Between 1850 and 1900, stagecoaches carried tens of thousands of passengers on regularly-scheduled routes across the West. Many prospective miners chose this method of travel because it was much quicker than traveling with a wagon train. Compared to modern transportation, however, a stagecoach trip was painfully uncomfortable and dreadfully slow.

A newspaper printed this advice to passengers in 1877: "Don't imagine for a moment you are going on a picnic; expect annoyance, discomfort and some hardships. If you are disappointed, thank heaven."

1. Rewrite this advice in your own words. _____

_____

_____

Passengers traveling long distances carried their own weapons, blankets, water, and food. The stagecoach continued traveling day and night, averaging five to ten miles an hour. Rough roads and hairpin turns made sleep almost impossible. One reporter wrote: "The jolting will be found disagreeable at first, but a few nights without sleep obviate that difficulty."

Relay stations every 10 to 25 miles provided rest stops. One passenger reported that "the available food would curdle a goat's stomach." Passengers also complained about the lack of toilet and bathing facilities at the rest stops.

Most passengers rode on wooden benches inside the stagecoach. Mail, baggage, and sometimes passengers rode on seats outside or on the roof. When the stagecoach came to a steep hill, mud, or soft sand, passengers had to get out and walk to lighten the load and sometimes even to help push. The trip from Missouri to California took about a month and cost $200.

Stagecoaches were not heated or cooled. A blind covered the window, but didn't completely block snow, rain, wind, or dust. Coaches designed to hold nine passengers might end up carrying 15 or 20. Overloaded stagecoaches had a tendency to overturn.

Passengers faced other dangers including runaway horses, bison stampedes, and attacks by robbers or Native Americans.

2. Would you have been willing to ride 2,000 miles on a stagecoach to reach the gold fields? Why or why not?

_____

_____

_____

Name: _____ Date: _____

Traveling By Sea

Many prospectors decided to reach California by booking passage on clipper ships. The trip around Cape Horn was long, dangerous, and expensive. Greedy ship captains signed up as many passengers as they could crowd onto a ship. People often slept three to a bed.

The supply of ships did not nearly meet the demand for travel, and many older ships that were barely seaworthy were brought into service.

Once ships reached California, the crews often deserted to join the Gold Rush. Ships were abandoned and left to rot.

This journey took about 100 days if everything went well. Strong currents, icebergs, and fierce winds off Cape Horn often caused ships to go off course, adding more time to the journey.

A second option was to sail across the Gulf of Mexico to Panama. From there, travelers walked or rode horses 100 miles through dense jungles to Panama City in the hopes of catching a ship heading north on the Pacific side.

This route was also uncertain, long, and dangerous. The food was terrible, and the water was thick, murky, and often filled with insects. Yellow fever, malaria, dysentery, and cholera prevented many prospective miners from reaching California.

1. How would you have felt if you were the captain of a ship whose crew had deserted?

   _____

   _____

   _____

2. Using the map on the next page, trace in red the route ships took from New York, around South America, to California.

3. Using the map on the next page, trace in blue the route a miner would have taken from New Orleans to Panama, and across Panama to California.

4. On another sheet of paper, make a poster from a fictional shipping company that exaggerates the conditions of travel to California and the promises of what people will find there.

Name: _____ Date: _____

Traveling By Sea Map

Use the map below to complete the activity on page 13.

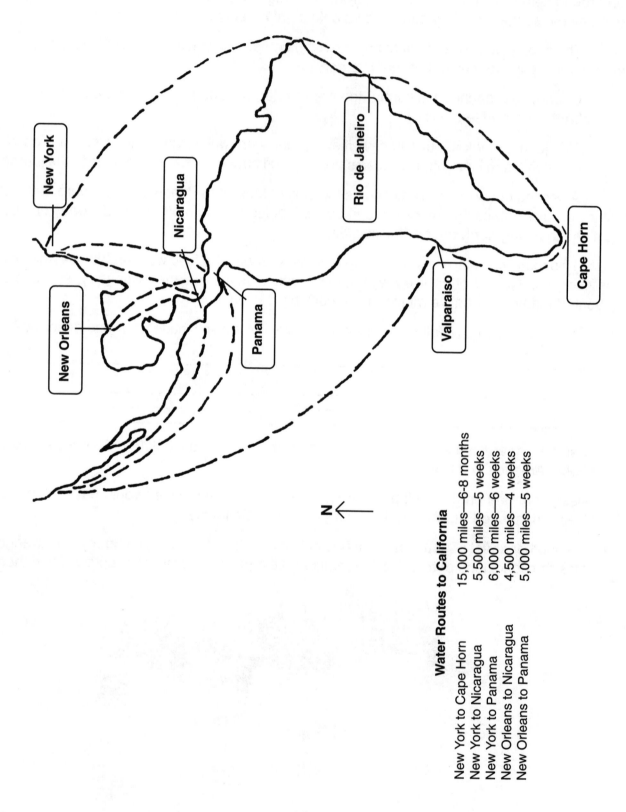

New York

Nicaragua

Rio de Janeiro

Cape Horn

New Orleans

Panama

Valparaiso

N ←

Water Routes to California

New York to Cape Horn   15,000 miles—6-8 months
New York to Nicaragua   5,500 miles—5 weeks
New York to Panama   6,000 miles—6 weeks
New Orleans to Nicaragua   4,500 miles—4 weeks
New Orleans to Panama   5,000 miles—5 weeks

Name: _____ Date: _____

Gold Rush Homonyms

Homonyms are words that sound alike but are spelled differently and have different meanings. **Example:** *miner* and *minor*

Write a homonym for each word listed on the line below the word, then write a short definition for each word.

1. karat _____

_____ _____

2. stake _____

_____ _____

3. mail _____

_____ _____

4. right _____

_____ _____

5. sea _____

_____ _____

6. poor _____

_____ _____

7. ore _____

_____ _____

8. sail _____

_____ _____

9. jeans _____

_____ _____

10. routes _____

_____ _____

Name: _____ Date: _____

Hardships and Danger

This song describes the hardships and dangers of the trip to California.

The Fools of Forty-Nine

When gold was found in forty-eight, the people said 'twas gas,
And some were fools enough to think the lumps were made of brass,
But they soon were satisfied and started off to mine,
They bought a ship came round the Horn in the fall of forty-nine.

CHORUS: Then they thought of what they had been told,
                    When they started after gold,
                    That they never in this world would make a pile.

The poor, the old, the rotten scows were advertised to sail
From New Orleans with passengers, but they must pump and bail.
The ships were crowded more than full, but some hung on behind,
And other dived off from the wharf and swam till they were blind.

CHORUS

With rusty pork and stinking beef and rotten wormy bread
With captains too that never were as high as the mainmast head,
The steerage passengers would rave and swear they'd paid their passage
They wanted something more to eat besides Bologna sausage.

CHORUS

And they begun to cross the plains with oxen, holler and 'haw;
And steamers they began to run as far as Panama,
And there for months the people stayed that started after gold,
And some returned disgusted with the lies they had been told.

CHORUS

The people died on every route, they sickened and died like sheep,
And those at sea before they were dead were launched into the deep,
And those that died crossing the Plains fared not as well as that,
For a hole was dug and they was dumped along the terrible Platte.

CHORUS

---

1. Select one verse from this song. On your own paper, rewrite it in your own words and explain what it means.

         16

Name: _____ Date: _____

Seeing the Elephant

To those who rushed to California, one expression characterized the trip more than any other: "seeing the elephant."

The expression goes back to a story about when circus parades first featured elephants. According to the story, a farmer heard the circus was in town. He had never seen an elephant and was very excited about the prospect. He loaded his wagon with vegetables to take to market, expecting to make a large profit.

On the way to town he met the circus parade, led by an elephant. The farmer was thrilled, but his horses were terrified. They bolted, overturned the wagon, and ruined the vegetables.

"I don't give a hang," said the farmer, "for I have seen the elephant."

1. What do you think the farmer meant by that? _____

_____

_____

Those who planned to travel West announced they were going to see the elephant.

2. What do you think they meant? _____

_____

_____

Those who went partway and turned back for any reason said they had seen "the elephant's tracks" or "the tail of the elephant."

3. What do you think they meant? _____

_____

_____

4. What would "seeing the elephant" be for you? _____

_____

_____

Name: _____ Date: _____

Too Good to Be True

"Don't believe everything you read" is good advice today. It was even better advice during the Gold Rush.

Three Weeks in the Gold Mines, written by Henry Simpson, claimed his partner had found a gold nugget "about as large and thick as my double hands outspread." It was a good story, but completely untrue. The title implied that people could quickly find large chunks of gold. Books like Simpson's caused even those with a mild case of gold fever to become strongly infected, ready to risk everything and rush to California.

Some of the guidebooks were authentic, however. They offered good advice, helpful tips, practical suggestions, and a realistic description of the journey and hardships.

Many of the useless guidebooks were written by armchair experts who had never been west of the Mississippi River.

Some guidebooks were downright dangerous because of the amount of inaccurate or false information they contained. They included hearsay and rumors reported as truth, parts of government documents, newspaper clippings, and inaccurate maps.

Some authors suggested the worst possible routes to take and underplayed the hardships of the journey. "The journey is one of the most delightful and invigorating," claimed one source.

1. Why do you think books like Simpson's were more likely to be read and believed than the ones that were realistic?

    _____

    _____

    _____

2. What is an "armchair expert"? _____

    _____

    _____

3. What does this saying mean to you? "If it sounds too good to be true, it probably is."

    _____

    _____

4. How can you apply this saying to your life? _____

    _____

    _____

Name: _____ Date: _____

Arriving at the Gold Fields

It might be difficult for people today to understand why men left homes, businesses, and families to travel thousands of miles in search of gold. The possibility of finding a huge fortune must have been very tempting to farmers who made only two or three hundred dollars during a good year. The same was true for factory workers who made about a dollar for working a

twelve-hour day. Even skilled craftsmen made only about a dollar and a half a day. Many felt it was worth taking the chance to travel to California where gold was free to anyone who could find it. Stories of miners becoming rich in a short time spread like wildfire. Many of these stories were exaggerations; however, some of them were actually true.

When prospectors finally arrived in California, they learned that conditions were not what they expected. For one thing, gold nuggets weren't simply sitting around waiting to be picked up.

Another big shock was the prices merchants charged for goods. Iron pans that miners needed to search for gold would have cost 20 cents before 1849. Instead, they sold for $8! The price of a horse went from $6 to over $300.

Food prices were also inflated. A loaf of bread cost $2; a pound of butter, $6; a tin of sardines, $16; and one egg, $3!

1. Besides hunting for gold, why else do you think people might have wanted to travel to California in 1849?

    _____

    _____

2. Use a dictionary. What does *inflation* mean? _____

    _____

3. How much would a dozen eggs have cost? _____

4. Why do you think merchants were able to charge such outrageous prices and get away with it?

    _____

    _____

Name: _____ Date: _____

Panning for Gold

Most early prospectors used a technique called "panning" to search for gold. The advantage of this method was that the cost of the equipment needed was minimal. As you read about panning for gold, note the disadvantages of this method and write them at the bottom of the page.

To pan for gold, a prospector had to kneel or stand at the side of or in a stream of running water. He reached down to the bottom of the stream with his pan and filled it about half full of dirt and gravel. Those without metal pans used baskets, tin cups, old hats, or blankets.

After he removed twigs and sticks from the pan, he let the pan fill with water. As he pulled the pan near the surface, he shook it back and forth, tapping it against the heel of his hand.

He then tilted the edge of the pan back and forth to allow a small amount of gravel to slip over the edge. He repeated this several times until the smallest amount of debris remained.

At this point, he may have spotted a flake or two of gold in the pan. When the pan contained almost no gravel, he swirled it gently. Because gold is much heavier than sand, it stays in the center while the sand moves to the outside.

Usually the pan yielded nothing but sand, but sometimes a miner could pick out a few specks of gold. To have any chance of finding even a small amount of gold, prospectors repeated this process over and over and over, from daybreak to dark, in good weather and bad.

As more and more miners arrived to search for gold, other methods were introduced that were more effective and faster than panning for gold.

1. Disadvantages of panning method: _____

_____

_____

_____

_____

_____

_____

_____

_____

Panning for Gold Activity

Parent/Teacher Directions: Let students experience first-hand what it was like to pan for gold. If possible, take students to a shallow creek or stream to make the experience as realistic as possible.

You can also set up your own "stream" outside where students can pan for gold. Have them wear old shoes and clothes and bring a change of shoes and clothes. They will probably get wet.

Students can use disposable aluminum pie tins for their pans.

Preparation: If you will be panning for gold in a creek or stream, no other preparations are needed unless you wish to "salt" the stream with small pieces of gravel, spray-painted to look like gold. Have students read and follow the directions for panning on the previous page.

To prepare your own "stream," you will need:

A large tub of cold water; *(Several tubs will allow more students to pan for gold at the same time.)*; several pails of coarse sand; and a handful of fine gravel, spray-painted to look like gold. Mix the "gold" thoroughly with the sand.

Directions: Have students place a small scoop of sand in their pans. Dip the pans in the "stream" (tubs of cold water). Follow the directions for panning on the previous page.

Panning for gold is more difficult than it may seem at first. Mastering this technique takes quite a bit of practice. Allow students to work at it for at least an hour. Students "strike it rich" if they find any gold gravel.

After they finish, have students write about the experience as though it were a journal entry written by a miner.

Name: _____ Date: _____

Rocking the Cradle

Panning for gold was slow, tedious, and not very effective. Prospectors wanted a faster way to gather the gold; some decided to try another technique.

When they found a likely place on the river, miners built a rocker. A rocker looked something like a baby cradle with a handle on one side. The rocker was made of two shallow wooden boxes, one on top of the other.

The upper box was about half as long as the lower one and had holes in it. The lower box had cleats called riffles across it and a hole at one end. Miners shoveled sand, silt, and gravel into the top box. Then they scooped up water and poured it over the top while they rocked the cradle (moved the rocker back and forth with the handle).

The rocking motion caused pebbles that were too large to fit through the holes to remain in the upper box. Mud and water ran through the holes into and out of the lower box. The cleats caught and held any particles of gold.

This method was most effective when two people worked together; while one shoveled in the material, the other poured in the water and rocked the box.

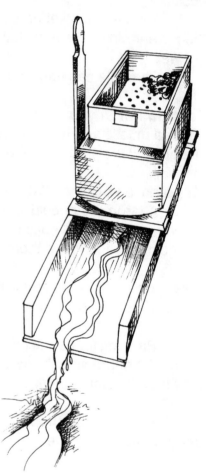

True or False?

Circle "T" for true or "F" for False.

1   T   F   Using a rocker was faster than panning for gold.

2.   T   F   Two people were needed to use a rocker.

3.   T   F   The lower box of the rocker was shorter than the upper one.

4.   T   F   When the miner pulled the handle, all the rocks and pebbles in the upper box fell out.

5.   T   F   The cleats in the lower box kept particles of gold from washing away.

Name: _____ Date: _____

Using a "Long Tom"

Another method of searching for gold was to build a "long tom." This also consisted of wooden boxes on two levels. Each box was about a foot and a half wide and about eight feet long. Both had one open end covered with a strainer. The closed ends were raised several inches higher than the open ends. Like rockers, the boxes had cleats or riffles that formed grooves or ridges to catch and hold gold particles.

To use a long tom, miners needed a constant source of running water. They could dig a trough to divert the water from a stream to the long tom or use pipes or hoses.

It took three people to work the long tom effectively. Two people shoveled muck from the river or stream into the top box, while a third person constantly stirred the muck to keep it from clogging up. As the material was washed away by the running water, small particles of gold could be caught in the cleats.

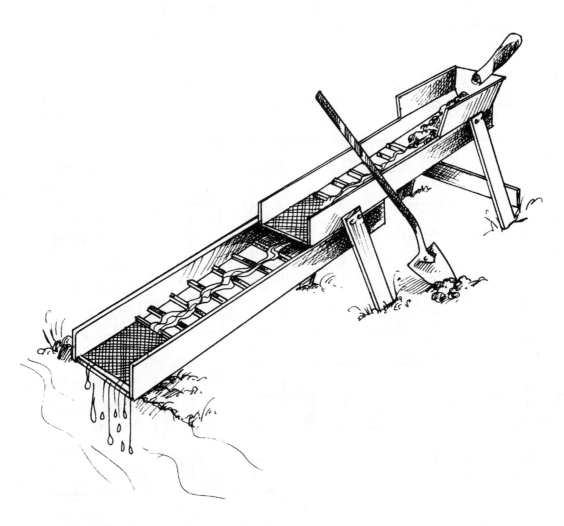

Name: _____ Date: _____

Sluicing for Gold

A sluice was similar to a long tom, except that it contained more wooden boxes and could be several hundred feet long. A sluice needed to be built across a sharp bend in a stream or river to connect the two parts of the stream and make the water detour across the riffles.

The miners shoveled dirt and gravel into the highest box and let the water wash it out of the sluice. Like rocker boxes and long toms, the riffles in the sluice caught the small particles of gold

1.   If you had been a "forty-niner," which method would you have pre-ferred: using a rocker box, a long tom, a sluice, or panning for gold? Why? Write your answers on your own paper.

Go for the Gold Puzzle

Unscramble each of the clues related to mining for gold. The last letter of one word will always become the first letter of the next word. To decode the puzzle, unscramble and write the shaded letters in the boxes below. The letters will spell out an exclamation used by miners when they discover gold.

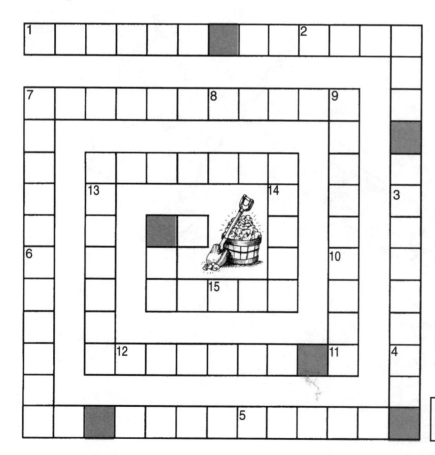

1.   RIANAOCIFL
2.   RATUANSGO
3.   CUSLEI
4.   ALENTPHE
5.   TKOOMEYRNSCMK
6.   SLOEHV
7.   GMOTOLN
8.   NRIEM
9.   KRERCO
10. RUHS
11. RSHHPADI
12. GNANIPN
13. TTONHSOGW
14. GGENUT
15. VTERAL

!

Name: _____ Date: _____

Tidbits of Gold Rush Trivia

- The first recorded discovery of gold in California occurred in 1842 when Don Francisco Lopez discovered the precious metal at Placeritas Canyon in the San Fernando Valley, about 40 miles northwest of Los Angeles. While digging onions, he noticed something glittering among the roots. Within a few weeks, hundreds of people went to the area to try their luck. The deposits were worked successfully for a number of years but were eventually depleted and forgotten.

- In 1914 a gold-lined geode was discovered at Cripple Creek, Colorado. It was 20 feet long, 5 feet wide, and 40 feet high!

- Between 1848 and 1856, about $465 million worth of gold was discovered in California. However, geologists have confirmed that the majority of gold is still there; as much as 85 percent of the gold remains. Each year, new veins are exposed as many geological changes take place, such as floods, earthquakes, droughts, freezing temperatures, and mud slides.

- Over a quarter of the world's annual gold production comes from the Transvaal Province of South Africa.

- Almost half of the world's gold (45 percent) is kept in safes and vaults. In Switzerland, the people who take care of the vaults are called the "gnomes of Zurich."

- The number of cattle in California went from less than 300,000 in 1848 to over 3 million by 1860.

- The Treaty of Guadalupe-Hidalgo ended the Mexican War. Mexico ceded all of California and other parts of the southwest to the United States in exchange for $15 million. The treaty was signed less than a month after James Marshall discovered gold.

- When the California constitution was written in 1849, Native Americans had no political or legal rights.

- The California Legislature passed a foreign miner's tax. Miners who were not U.S. citizens had to pay a monthly fee of $20 for the right to mine for gold.

1. Use reference sources to find two other interesting bits of Gold Rush trivia.

_____

_____

_____

_____

Name: _____ Date: _____

Shantytowns and Boomtowns

Whenever a quantity of gold was discovered in a new area, hundreds rushed there to try their luck. Small communities sprang up almost overnight. Miners lived in tents and rickety shacks, called shanties. If there wasn't much gold in the area, the "shantytown" disappeared as quickly as it began, often even before it had been named.

If the gold strike was a big one, a "boomtown" grew quickly. Homes and buildings for doctors, bankers, blacksmiths, and merchants sprang up among the tents and shacks. Many small towns boomed for a time during the California Gold Rush but then were deserted once the gold played out in the area.

The biggest, wildest boomtown in California was San Francisco. The population increased by 25,000 in two years. At one time, an average of 30 houses a day were being built. Besides homes, businesses, saloons, and gambling houses sprang up.

Although San Francisco continued to flourish after the Gold Rush, many boomtowns were deserted. Abandoned boomtowns soon became ghost towns. Remains of some of these towns have become popular tourist attractions.

1. Why do you think miners lived in tents and shanties rather than building nice homes?

   _____

   _____

2. What is the difference between a "shantytown" and a "boomtown"?

   _____

   _____

3. Take a mental field trip to a ghost town one year after it was abandoned. Stand in the middle of the street. Look around you and describe the ghost town in detail.

   • What do you see? _____

   _____

   • What do you hear? _____

   _____

   • What do you smell? _____

   _____

   • How do you feel about what you observe? _____

   _____

Name: _____ Date: _____

Gold Rush Towns

Of the thousands of mining camps that arose during the years of the Gold Rush, most have disappeared without a trace. Towns like Hell-out-for-Noon City, Slumgullion, Delirium Tremens, Bogus Thunder, Graveyard, Mugfuzzle Flat, and Hell's Delight are only memories from diaries, newspapers, and maps.

1. Select one of the towns shown on the map and write a short story on another sheet of paper about how it might have gotten its name.

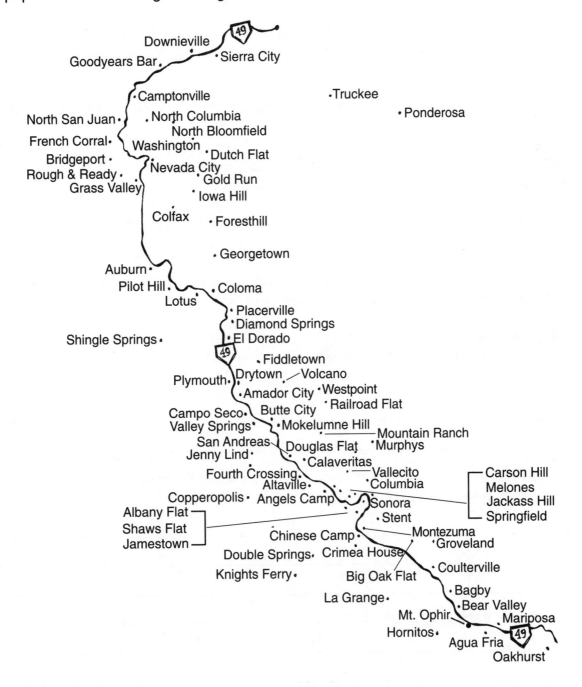

Name: _____ Date: _____

Staking a Claim

Until gold was discovered in California, there were no laws regarding mining. As the forty-niners rushed to the area, a series of informal "codes" was established in mining camps.

When a miner found traces of gold, he could stake a "claim" to the area. This gave him the exclusive right to search for gold there, but it did not give him ownership of the land. Claims were limited to one per person. If no one worked a claim for a week, it became available to anyone else who wanted to claim it.

The size of a claim varied. In some mining camps, a claim was limited to 10 square feet. In others, the limit was 50 square feet. "Jumping" a claim (taking over someone else's claim by force) happened frequently.

Claims officers were paid by miners. They patrolled the area, settled disputes, and over-saw the buying and selling of sites.

Sometimes swindlers "salted" a claim. They scattered a small amount of gold dust in the dirt and then sold their claims for large amounts of money.

Where no mining camps existed, miners tried to claim large areas of land. However, if word of a gold strike leaked out, it was impossible for one person to defend a large area.

1. Imagine the sidewalk is a stream. Have each member of the class mark an area equal to 10 square feet along both sides of the sidewalk and stand in their "claim."

2. Write what you think it would have been like to spend as much as 18 hours a day in this small area surrounded by other miners, all panning for gold.

   _____

   _____

   _____

3. Why do you think it was in the miners' best interest to follow the codes in mining camps even if they weren't legally enforced?

   _____

   _____

   _____

4. Why do you think people salted claims? _____

   _____

   _____

Name: _____ Date: _____

Read All About It

Read a fiction book about someone who prospected for gold. Fill in the information below.

1. When did the story take place? _____

2. Briefly describe two of the main characters. _____

_____

_____

3. Where were the main characters originally from? _____

4. What were their occupations before becoming miners? _____

_____

5. Why did they become miners? _____

_____

_____

6. Describe the route taken to the gold fields. _____

_____

7. What was the name of the mining camp? _____

8. Did they find gold? _____

9. Did they become wealthy? If yes, how? If not, why not? _____

_____

_____

10. Summarize one adventure they had in the story. _____

_____

_____

11. How did the story end? _____

_____

12. Did you like the book? Why or why not? _____

_____

Suggested Fiction:

Around the Great Horn Spoon by Sid Fleischman
Gold Rush Phoebe by Kathleen Karn
Boom Town by Sonia Levitin

Name: _____ Date: _____

Prices: Then and Now

Food prices in the gold fields of California were much higher than anywhere else in the United States at that time.

1. List two reasons why you think prices were so high. _____
_____

2. Compare the prices of these items during the Gold Rush to prices today. Calculate the difference between then and now.

ITEM	GOLD RUSH PRICES	PRICES TODAY	DIFFERENCE
Bread	$2/loaf (At restaurants, bread sold for $1 a slice.)		
Butter	$6/pound		
Cheese	$8/pound		
Onions	$1.50/pound		
Tin of Sardines	$16 each		
Eggs	$3 each ($36 a dozen)		
Flour	$1/pound		
Coffee	$4/pound		
Dried Beans	$1/pound		
Sugar	$2/pound		

3. For each shopping list, calculate the cost then and now:

List A: 1# cheese
1# butter
1 loaf of bread
1# beans
Total then: _____
Total now: _____

List B: 5# flour
1 dozen eggs
1 tin of sardines
2# coffee
2# onions
Total then: _____
Total now: _____

Name: _____ Date: _____

Getting Rich

Early in the California Gold Rush, prospectors could expect to find about an ounce of gold in creeks and rivers on a given day. Since gold was worth $16 an ounce, this didn't amount to a vast fortune for most miners. Although reports of the amount of gold available and the number of big strikes were exaggerated, many miners did become very wealthy.

Some California miners accomplished what they set out to do—they struck it rich and took home a fortune. Those lucky few paid off mortgages on their farms and started new lives.

Not everyone who got rich during the California Gold Rush did it by mining for gold, however. Some gave up mining but stayed in California to open businesses in the boomtowns or to farm the fertile valleys.

Some made money in other ways. Gamblers found it was easier to extract gold from the pockets of gullible miners than to dig for it in the gold fields. Con men sold useless items at inflated prices.

Merchants charged miners outlandish prices for supplies and services. Sugar sold for $2 a pound, and coffee was $4 a pound. Men and women earned $50 a week doing laundry. Restaurants charged $25 or more for meals.

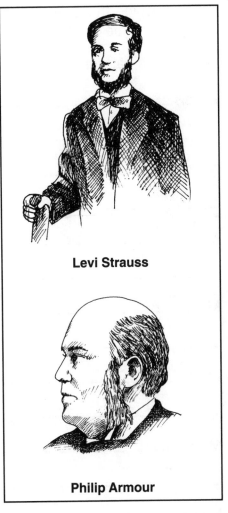

Levi Strauss

Philip Armour

In 1849, those prices were sky-high. Successful miners could easily pay them, but many miners could barely make ends meet.

Two men who got their start in the boomtowns of California were Levi Strauss and Philip Armour. Armour made his fortune by opening a butcher shop and supplying meat to the miners. His business grew until he eventually became the largest supplier of beef in the United States.

1. Levi Strauss became successful selling something the miners needed for daily use. What did Levi Strauss sell?

_____

2. Use reference sources to write a short report on your own paper about Levi Strauss or Philip Armour, describing how they made their fortunes during the California Gold Rush.

Name: _____ Date: _____

What Would They Have Said?

Imagine the conversation between a miner who is down on his luck and in need of supplies and the owner of a general store who is unwilling to advance credit without collateral.

Work with a partner to write a dialog between these two people.

Miner: _____

_____

Merchant: _____

_____

Miner: _____

_____

Merchant: _____

_____

Miner: _____

_____

Merchant: _____

_____

Miner: _____

_____

Merchant: _____

_____

Miner: _____

_____

Merchant: _____

_____

Name: _____ Date: _____

Gold Rush Justice

Most types of gold mining required the cooperation of two or more people. People formed partnerships to build and operate rockers, long toms, and sluices. Arguments arose over how to split the profits. Many disputes ended in fights or even murder.

There were no official law enforcement agents in the gold fields of California. At the height of the Gold Rush, about two murders a day were committed in San Francisco alone.

California was part of Mexico until the end of the Mexican War in 1848. Although the area was legally administered by the U.S. Army after that, there was no formal government until California became a state in 1850. Even then people were more interested in prospecting than in becoming part of a legal system that would take time away from their search for gold.

As soon as word of a new gold strike leaked out, hundreds of miners rushed to the area. They staked nearby claims, hoping to collect a share of the wealth. Sometimes the person who had staked the original claim was murdered, and others took over the claim.

The Gold Rush town of Bodie, high in the Sierras, gained a reputation as the most lawless mining town in the West. The local newspaper even published a column titled "Last Night's Killings."

In many cases, people took the law into their own hands. Without courts, lawyers, judges, and juries, justice wasn't always fair; it could be swift and merciless. When vigilante groups captured someone accused of a crime, he might be punished without a trial.

Robbery also became a major problem. Not only did people steal gold, they also stole equipment, firewood, horses, and even food from each other. In 1851, the California legislature passed a law allowing the death penalty for stealing property worth more than $100. Banishment, cutting off a person's ears, branding, and whipping, as well as hanging, were common forms of punishment.

1. Use a dictionary. Define *vigilante*. _____

   _____

2. Greed was the dominant motive for crimes during the California Gold Rush. Do you agree or disagree with this statement? Explain your answer.

   _____

   _____

   _____

   _____

Name: _____   Date: _____

"The Wickedest Town in the West"

High in the Sierras, summers are cool. Rain is rare except for occasional violent thunderstorms. Winters bring strong winds, subzero temperatures, and 20 feet of snow. Not much grows there other than sagebrush. Although it is not a sunny California town, over 10,000 people once lived in Bodie, California.

In the fall of 1859, Bill Bodey began exploring for gold in the area with three partners. One story claims Bodey chased a wounded rabbit into a hole. While trying to get at the rabbit, he discovered gold.

The partners knew how treacherous winter could be, so they decided to wait until the following spring to work the claim. Bodey couldn't wait. He and another man returned, built a cabin, and continued to explore the area. In November the two men were caught in a blizzard. His partner made it back to the cabin, but Bodey didn't. His body wasn't found until the following spring.

Rich strikes in places with better weather drew attention away from Bodie for a time. Then in 1876, a rich vein of gold was discovered, and the rush to Bodie began. By the following year, the town had grown to 2,000. Another gold strike in 1878 caused the population to swell to over 10,000. Crime increased as quickly as the population of Bodie.

With so many people arriving so quickly, nearly everything was in short supply. Because of its location, all supplies, including lumber and firewood, had to be brought in by freight wagons. At times, the severe weather prevented anyone from getting into or out of the area for long periods.

After a long series of assaults, robberies, and murders, citizens of the city decided enough was enough. On January 14, 1881, a mob lynched a man accused of murder. From then on, the vigilante group kept some semblance of order in the town that had earned the nickname "the wickedest town in the West."

Today, Bodie is a California state historic park. Only tourists wander down Main Street now. The deserted buildings are silent and so is the cemetery where so many dreams are buried.

Imagine that you have recently arrived in California from the east coast after a long, difficult journey that lasted almost a year. Hearing about the gold found in Bodie, your family decides to continue on and settle there. You've heard about the weather and the crime in Bodie, as well as the stories of fantastic amounts of gold found there.

1. On another sheet of paper, write a letter to a friend telling how you feel about moving to Bodie, California.

Name: _____ Date: _____

Black Bart

One of California's better-known Gold Rush villains, Charles E. Bolton (a.k.a. Black Bart), was responsible for 28 Wells Fargo Stagecoach robberies.

**Charles E. Bolton
(a.k.a. "Black Bart")**

Black Bart was probably born in New York City and migrated to California about 1830. His real name may have been Charles Bole. He tried his luck as a farmer, a peddler of patent medicines, and a prospector, before turning to robbery.

Black Bart's first hold-up in 1877 near Fort Ross wasn't very profitable. The strongbox contained $300 in cash and a $300 check.

Stories about Black Bart claimed he never robbed individual passengers. He was nicknamed "the gentleman bandit" because he said "please" and "thank you" when robbing a stage. He even politely called the driver "Sir."

Black Bart soon became a celebrity in local newspapers. When he left his first bit of poetry in an emptied strongbox, he became a legend.

For a time, authorities couldn't find any clues to Black Bart's identity. He wore a flour sack over his head and a full-length linen duster during robberies.

Black Bart eluded captivity until 1883 when he cut his hand trying to open a strongbox. Distracted by an approaching rider, he dropped the handkerchief he was using to wipe off the blood. The laundry mark on the handkerchief led investigators to Charles E. Bolton of San Francisco.

When he was finally arrested, people were surprised to learn he was 57 years old. They also discovered that his shotgun hadn't even contained shells when he robbed the stagecoaches.

1. What does *a.k.a.* mean? _____

2. Why do you think people make "heroes" out of people who are criminals?

   _____

   _____

3. Use reference sources: What is a laundry mark? _____

   _____

4. How would a laundry mark help authorities discover Black Bart's identity?

   _____

   _____

Name: _____ Date: _____

Tommyknockers

The Welsh had been miners for many years before the California Gold Rush. When Welsh miners traveled to California, they brought along some colorful stories and legends about Tommyknockers.

According to the legends, Tommyknockers were gnomes who lived in the mines. If the supports in a mine were about to collapse, the Tommyknockers tapped on the wooden beams to warn miners of danger. According to the stories, the gnomes cared for the safety of the miners, and the warnings gave miners an opportunity to escape.

Miners often heard knocking sounds in the mines caused by the slow buckling of support beams prior to a cave-in. When they heard that sound, they knew they had to get to safety fast.

1. What if Tommyknockers were real? Write a short story about friendly gnomes who warn people of danger by knocking on wood. Use a setting other than a gold mine for your story. Make yourself one of the characters in the story. Use another sheet of paper if you need more room.

_____

_____

_____

_____

_____

_____

_____

_____

_____

_____

Name: _____ Date: _____

Gold Rush Similes and Metaphors

A **simile** is a figure of speech that uses *like* or *as* to compare two things that are not alike.
Example: The miners along the stream were **as thick as flies**.

A **metaphor** is a figure of speech that uses a noun or noun phrase to make a direct comparison between two unlike things. The words *like* and *as* are not used in a metaphor.
Example: The man was **a bundle of nerves** when he arrived in San Francisco.

Write "M" for metaphor or "S" for simile on the line before each sentence.

1. _____ Their journey was a nightmare.

2. _____ The newspaper claimed that gold was as common as pebbles.

3. _____ The miner was as proud as a peacock when he found gold.

4. _____ His loneliness was a lump in his belly.

5. _____ His empty stomach growled like a grizzly bear.

Finish the similes.

6. The miner was as poor as _____.

7. The stagecoach ride was as rough as _____.

8. The ships to California were as _____.

9. Riding a mule was like _____.

10. Standing in the stream all day, the miner's feet were as _____.

Finish the metaphors.

11. The miner's happiness was _____.

12. The gold he found was _____.

13. His dented pan was a _____.

14. The discovery of gold was _____.

15. Gold fever turned him into a _____.

Name: _____ Date: _____

What Miners Wore

Shirts: Most miners wore a basic cotton work shirt. This type of shirt is still available at many stores today. Miners also wore red wool overshirts, winter and summer.

Pants: Miners, like other working men of the day, primarily wore cotton duck (canvas) or wool pants that came in different styles. The "drop front" design was popular since zippers hadn't been invented yet.

Belts: Although pants didn't have belt loops until the late 1800s, a miner usually wore a belt. This was not to hold up his pants, but rather as a place to hang items to keep them handy, like a pistol, knife, or gold pouch.

Boots: Miners bought the best leather boots they could afford. Good boots were needed as protection from sharp rocks, mud, and water. Miners were particularly thankful for good boots when a pick or shovel landed on a foot instead of rock.

Hats: Hats were essential for miners who spent many hours outside in the hot sun or cold rain. No one style was preferred, but common styles include the three shown here.

Mexican War Wheel Cap   **Beaver Felt Low Topper**   **Palm Leaf Panama**

Scarves: A large triangular cotton "kerchief" was also an essential part of every miner's costume.

Rubberized clothing: By 1849, a process was used to coat cloth with rubber. Rubber hat covers, raincoats, and blankets helped keep miners dry in most weather.

1. Why do you think the basic work shirt worn by miners is still worn today?

_____

_____

2. If you had been a miner, which type of hat would you have preferred? Why?

_____

_____

3. List several uses for a miner's kerchief. _____

_____

_____

Name: _____ Date: _____

Tools of the Trade

Canteens: Miners usually chose metal canteens made of tin and covered in buckskin or cloth because they were lighter than wooden canteens.

Lamps: Miners could purchase candleholders (open or enclosed) or oil lamps to provide light. Candles and lamp oil were very expensive.

Pouches: Most miners kept their gold dust or nuggets in a soft leather pouch. The pouch was quite long, so one end could be tucked securely through the belt.

Scales: Many miners carried portable scales to accurately measure their daily "take" and to assure that they were not being cheated when they exchanged their gold dust and nuggets for money.

Picks: Miners used picks to break up rocks and hard clumps of dirt.

Shovels: Shovels came in a variety of shapes, sizes, and styles. The most popular shovel during the Gold Rush era was the Ames shovel made in North Eaton, Massachusetts.

Cookware and eating utensils: Miners carried only the bare essentials for cooking and eating. Meals were prepared in a metal pot. A tin pot for coffee or tea, a metal fork and knife, a tin plate to eat from, and a sturdy tin cup were all a miner needed to cook and eat meals.

1. What is buckskin? _____

   _____

2. Draw a picture of a pick.

3. Compare what the miners used for cooking and eating to what most people use today.

   _____

   _____

   _____

Name: _____ Date: _____

Doctor, Doctor

When miners got sick, there were few doctors or medicines available. Most doctors charged outrageous fees for their services. Some diseases that are rare today were common then and were sometimes fatal. Even a toothache could be a major problem if there were no dentists in the area.

1. Use reference sources to learn more about any two of these diseases: cholera, influenza, diphtheria, malaria, scurvy, dysentery.

A. Disease: _____

   Symptom(s): _____

   _____

   Effects of disease: _____

   _____

   Cure(s): _____

   _____

   Prevention: _____

   _____

   Other Information: _____

   _____

B. Disease: _____

   Symptom(s): _____

   _____

   Effects of disease: _____

   _____

   Cure(s): _____

   _____

   Prevention: _____

   _____

   Other Information: _____

   _____

Name: _____ Date: _____

Interview a Miner

You are a reporter for an Eastern newspaper. Your boss sent you to California to interview a miner and write an article about the California Gold Rush. What is the name, age, and former occupation of the person you will interview?

_____

Write 12 questions you might ask that person during an interview.

1. _____
   _____

2. _____
   _____

3. _____
   _____

4. _____
   _____

5. _____
   _____

6. _____
   _____

7. _____
   _____

8. _____
   _____

9. _____
   _____

10. _____
   _____

11. _____
   _____

12. _____
   _____

Name: _____ Date: _____

From a Sleepy Village to a Large City

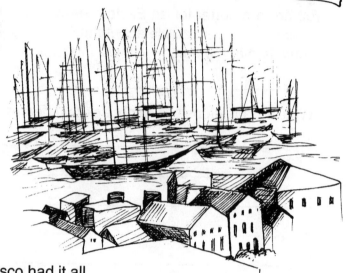

San Francisco was only a sleepy village on the Pacific coast before the Gold Rush. It grew from about 800 people in 1848, to 15,000 by 1849, and 25,000 one year later, becoming one of the fastest-growing cities in the world. By 1856, San Francisco had more than 50,000 citizens and was the largest and most important city in the West.

Ships carrying merchandise, supplies, and miners to California usually landed in San Francisco. Gold being shipped back east went out through that city. Miners bought their supplies, banked their gold, collected their mail, and came for recreation and relaxation. San Francisco had it all.

When cities grow quickly, they tend to be crowded, dirty, and poorly planned. San Francisco was no exception. From a field of canvas tents and wooden shacks, a town of houses and businesses grew almost overnight. Prefabricated houses shipped to San Francisco could be assembled in a day.

Abandoned ships clogged the harbor, deserted by their crews who ran off to hunt for gold. Material from some ships was scavenged for building. Many of the ships simply rotted away in the harbor.

Most streets were unpaved, and few had sidewalks. When it rained, mud and potholes made some streets impassible. A terrible fire broke out in May 1851; in just ten hours, it destroyed 2,000 homes and much of the business district.

Gradually new buildings of brick replaced the wooden ones. Places for rent were vastly overpriced. Labor was scare. Wages were high and so was the cost of living. The price of houses skyrocketed to $75,000. The price of food, supplies, and services increased as much as 1,000 percent.

Rats infested the city. Cats sold for $16 each. Robberies were common. Most men carried weapons for protection, especially after dark on the unlit streets.

Saloons became the social centers of the city, where people conducted business, drank, gambled, and were entertained by musicians and dancers.

Almost anyone willing to work could find a way to make money in San Francisco at that time.

1. If you had lived in San Francisco in 1849, what type of work would you have wanted to do? Why would that have been a good way to earn money? Write your answer on your own paper.

       42

Name: _____ Date: _____

Cause and Effect

A **cause** is an event that produces a result. An **effect** is the result produced.

For each cause, write an effect.

1. **Cause:** James Marshall discovered gold.

   Effect: _____

   _____

2. **Cause:** The Mexican War ended.

   Effect: _____

   _____

3. **Cause:** Some miners became very wealthy.

   Effect: _____

   _____

4. **Cause:** Tens of thousands of miners traveled to California in 1849.

   Effect: _____

   _____

5. **Cause:** Prices in California were very high during the Gold Rush era.

   Effect: _____

   _____

6. **Cause:** Crime was high in mining camps.

   Effect: _____

   _____

7. **Cause:** During the Gold Rush, San Francisco became one of the fastest-growing cities in the world.

   Effect: _____

   _____

8. **Cause:** When there was no more gold left in an area, miners moved on to other sites.

   Effect: _____

   _____

The Rest of the Story

Although James Marshall discovered the first gold on property owned by John Sutter, neither man profited from the discovery. Squatters overran the property Sutter had hoped to turn into an agriculture-based empire.

Sutter's 50,000 acres of land were invaded and ruined by prospectors searching for gold. They trampled his crops, muddied the streams, and killed his cattle for food.

"The country swarmed with lawless men," wrote John Sutter. "Talking with them did no good. I was alone and there was no law."

With his dreams of an agricultural empire crushed, Sutter tried his luck mining but never struck it rich. Years later he traveled to Washington, D.C., to ask Congress to recognize his claim to the land he had received from Mexico. While waiting for the decision, Sutter died in a Washington, D.C., hotel room on June 18, 1880.

James Marshall became famous for discovering gold at Sutter's mill, but like Sutter, he never became wealthy from that discovery. He tried prospecting, but like Sutter, he never located another rich strike. Marshall was forced to sell his own small ranch to pay off debts.

Marshall grew fruit and produced wines and brandies but failed after a few years. He tried prospecting again, bought into a partnership in a worthless mine, and even went on a lecture tour to raise money.

In 1872, the California State Legislature provided a two-year renewable pension for Marshall in recognition of his role in the state's history. Legend has it that when he went before the legislature in 1878 to ask for another renewal, a brandy bottle dropped out of his pocket, and the pension was denied. James Marshall died in poverty in 1885.

1. On another sheet of paper, write a letter that could have been written in 1880 by James Marshall or John Sutter to the other man. In the letter, have the writer talk about his life since 1848 and how he feels about his role in the Gold Rush.

Name: _____ Date: _____

Women Strike It Rich

Although men were the ones first infected with gold fever, women caught it, too. When women began arriving in California, they were welcomed enthusiastically, since the overwhelming majority of the first wave of prospectors were men. Some women tried mining for gold, but most found they could make as much as or more than most miners by using their practical skills.

Any woman who could cook was able to earn money serving food with a minimum of equipment. A board across a pair of saw-horses could serve as a table. If she didn't have enough cups, plates, or silverware, the miners shared.

If a woman could bake biscuits, bread, cakes, or pies, fry steak and eggs, or make stew or soup, she was almost guaranteed more customers than she could handle. Even with the high cost of ingredients, miners were willing to pay for "home-cooked" meals.

Other women found they could earn good money by sewing, mending, washing, ironing, and cleaning. Some women ran boardinghouses or hotels. The census of 1850 showed 23 women living in Nevada City, California. Of them, 12 took in boarders or ran hotels with their husbands, and three others worked in family taverns that took in boarders.

At that time, many people believed that women had a "civilizing" influence on men. When women lived in a community, schools, churches, and benevolent societies were soon estab-lished.

California was the first state to allow women to own property in their own name. (In other states, everything a woman had before marriage or earned afterwards belonged to her hus-band.) This encouraged many women to settle in California.

1. Why do you think men would rather pay high prices for meals cooked by women than to cook for themselves?

    _____

    _____

2. Use reference sources. What is a boardinghouse? What services did the person who ran the boardinghouse provide?

    _____

    _____

3. Do you agree that women have a "civilizing" influence on men? Why or why not?

    _____

    _____

Name: _____ Date: _____

Consequences

Before the Gold Rush of 1849, the area that became the state of California was sparsely settled. The Gold Rush transformed not only the lives of people but also California itself. California's population grew dramatically. Its towns, cities, and businesses thrived. Almost overnight, it became the most famous American state. People around the world knew the story of California, the golden land where a fortune could be dug from the ground.

Many of those who set off for California to find fame and fortune found hardship or death instead. Many never made it to California at all, dying during the 15,000-mile voyage around South America, as they crossed the jungles of Panama, or during the 2,000-mile overland trip from Missouri. Of those who did make it to California, many fell victim to disease, violence, or murder. Many of the women and children waiting back east never saw their loved ones again or ever found out what had happened to them.

About 200,000 Native Americans lived in California before 1849. They were isolated from the rest of the United States by mountain ranges and deserts. Although many different tribes lived there, each remained separate from the others. For the most part, they were Stone Age people. They had no domesticated beasts of burden, little formal government, no metal tools, and no written language. They hunted with bows and stone-tipped arrows. They used nets, hooks, and harpoons for fishing. They also gathered grasses, herbs, nuts, roots, seeds, and berries for food.

Not all the gold found in California was taken from streams. Much of the gold in California was buried deep underground (and still is). When the forty-niners left, mining companies moved in with work crews and large machinery.

Hydraulic mining was a method used to explore for gold in the soil of older, dried riverbeds. Powerful jets of water were sprayed against the land to wash out the gold. This type of mining caused much environmental damage. The landscape was pocked and rutted; rivers were clogged with the runoff silt. Hydraulic mining was banned in 1884.

1. Select a topic related to the consequences of the Gold Rush for a presentation. Include a written report and visual aids, such as a poster, collage, graph, demonstration, or diorama.

   Possible topics are:

   - The environmental impact of the California Gold Rush

   - The effect of the Gold Rush on one group of Native Americans in California

   - The effect of the Gold Rush on the demographics of California

Name: _____ Date: _____

True or False?

Circle "T" for True or "F" for False.

1. T   F   James Marshall was the first person to discover gold in California.

2. T   F   Most towns that began during the California Gold Rush eventually became large modern cities in California.

3. T   F   James Marshall discovered gold on property owned by John Sutter.

4. T   F   A series of boxes used by miners to search for gold were called "long johns."

5. T   F   Black Bart's real name was Charles E. Bolton.

6. T   F   John Sutter died a wealthy man thanks to the discovery of gold on his property.

7. T   F   Traveling by ship to California was an easy, inexpensive way to get to California.

8. T   F   Miners' pants did not have belt loops or zippers because those two items hadn't been invented yet.

9. T   F   People who rushed to the gold fields of California were called forty-niners because the average age of the miners was 49.

10. T   F   Miners from Wales were nicknamed Tommyknockers.

11. T   F   Bodie, California, was nicknamed "the wickedest town in the West."

12. T   F   Because there were so many miners in California, the prices of food and supplies were very reasonable.

13. List three techniques miners used to search for gold.

_____

_____

_____

_____

Name: _____   Date: _____

The Lousy Miner

This song, sung during the Gold Rush years, tells much about the life of unsuccessful miners. On your own paper, rewrite each verse in your own words. (Hint: *Lousy* has more than one meaning.)

The Lousy Miner

It's four long years since I reached this land,
In search of gold among the rocks and sand;
And yet I'm poor when the truth is told.
     I'm a lousy miner,
     I'm a lousy miner in search of shining gold.

I've lived on swine till I grunt and squeal,
No one can tell how my bowels feel,
With slapjacks a-swimming in bacon grease.
     I'm a lousy miner,
     I'm a lousy miner in search of shining gold.

I was covered with lice coming on the boat,
I threw away my fancy swallow-tailed coat,
And now they crawl up and down my back.
     I'm a lousy miner,
     I'm a lousy miner in search of shining gold.

My sweetheart vowed she'd wait for me
Till I returned; but don't you see
She's married now, sure, so I'm told,
     Left her lousy miner,
     Left her lousy miner, in search of shining gold.

Oh, land of gold, you did me deceive,
And I intend in thee my bones to leave;
So farewell home, now I grow cold,
     I'm a lousy miner,
     I'm a lousy miner in search of shining gold.

48

Name: _____ Date: _____

Fact or Opinion?

A fact is a statement that can be verified as true.
Fact: James Marshall discovered gold in California.

An opinion is a statement that cannot be verified as true.
Opinion: James Marshall was a very lucky man.

Write "F" for fact or "O" for opinion on the line by each statement.

_____ 1. Gold was discovered in California in 1848.

_____ 2. People who rushed to California in search of gold were foolish.

_____ 3. Gold is prettier than silver.

_____ 4. Gold is more valuable than silver.

_____ 5. Bodie, California, was called "the wickedest town in the west."

_____ 6. Bodie, California, was the most wicked town in the west.

_____ 7. Miners who lived in shanties were too lazy to build real houses.

_____ 8. Women didn't become miners because they didn't like to get their hands dirty.

_____ 9. Vigilantes had the right to take justice in their own hands because of the high crime rate during the Gold Rush.

_____ 10. The population of San Francisco grew quickly because of the Gold Rush.

11. Write one fact about the California Gold Rush.

_____

_____

_____

12. Write one opinion about the California Gold Rush.

_____

_____

_____

Name: _____ Date: _____

Matching

Match the words in the box with their definitions.

alloy	**boomtown**	**bullion**	**claim**
density	**forty-niner**	**inflation**	**karat**
kerchief	**long tom**	**nugget**	**pick**
prospector	**shanty**	**vigilantes**	

_____ 1. A mixture of two or more metals

_____ 2. A lump of precious metal

_____ 3. Measurement of mass per unit volume

_____ 4. Measurement of the purity of gold

_____ 5. A solid bar of a precious metal

_____ 6. A town that grew suddenly near a gold strike

_____ 7. A piece of land worked by a miner

_____ 8. A person who went to California in 1849 in search of gold

_____ 9. A long box used to separate dirt and rocks from gold

_____ 10. A shack

_____ 11. People who took the law into their own hands

_____ 12. A miner

_____ 13. A tool used to break up rocks or clumps of dirt

_____ 14. A scarf worn by miners

_____ 15. A large increase in prices

_____ 16. Which picture shows a rocker?

A.
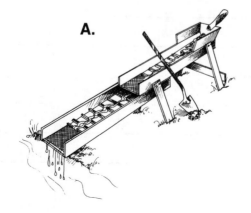

B.
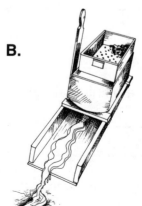

Name: _____ Date: _____

There's Gold Here

Many words and phrases contain the word gold (or golden). Use a dictionary or other reference source to answer these questions.

1. In the Olympics, a gold medal is given to which winner of an event: first, second, or third place? _____

2. Another name for "fool's gold" is _____.

3. Goldenrod is a _____.

4. What type of fish is a goldfish? _____

5. Which state is nicknamed the "Golden State"? _____

6. Another term for "golden years" is _____.

7. What type of animal is a goldfinch? _____

8. A golden anniversary is celebrated when a couple has been married _____ years.

9. The name of the little girl in the story of "The Three Bears" was _____.

10. A person who makes jewelry and other items from gold is called a _____.

11. If a person is accused of being a goldbrick, what does that mean? _____

12. What is the name of the famous bridge in California that crosses San Francisco Bay?

_____

13. What country is called the Gold Coast? _____

14. What is a "golden oldie"? _____

Write two other words or phrases that contain the word gold. Write a short definition for each.

15. _____
_____

16. _____
_____

Name: _____ Date: _____

They Came From Around the World

During the first wave of the Gold Rush, Americans worked side by side with miners from South America, Mexico, Asia, and Europe. As gold became more difficult to find, American miners began to resent the presence of "foreigners" and felt they shouldn't be allowed to take a share of "American gold" found on "American soil." This prejudice also included American Blacks and Native Americans of California.

By 1852, 20,000 Chinese peasants had made the treacherous 6,000 mile voyage to search for California gold. When finding good claims became more difficult, many mining camps banned all "Asiatics" and "South Sea Islanders" (Hawaiians). Sometimes the prejudice turned to violence.

For self-protection, groups of Chinese established their own mining camps. For the most part, they were hard workers, often finding gold where others had failed. Using a device called a "Chinese waterwheel" enabled them to drain streams and uncover gold.

Mexican miners were especially disliked by former soldiers who had recently fought in the Mexican War. That dislike extended to all Spanish-speaking miners.

Mexican and Chilean miners were successful in the southern mines in 1849 and 1850, using a technique called *winnowing*. Winnowing meant shaking blankets filled with dirt until only gold remained.

In 1850, the California legislature passed a law requiring all foreign miners to pay a $20 monthly fee "... for the privilege of taking from our country the vast treasure to which they have no right."

Winnowing

Write the answers on your own paper.

1. Prejudice also existed against Europeans, but not as strongly as the feelings against the Chinese, Mexicans, and South Americans. Why do you think this was the case?

2. What is your opinion of the way American miners reacted to foreigners?

3. How do you think you might have reacted if you were an unsuccessful miner and foreigners around you were finding gold?

4. Write three reasons that could have been used by a foreigner to explain why he had as much right to search for gold as Americans did.

52

Name: _____ Date: _____

In the News

A newspaper headline is a summary of the most important point in an article. Headlines must be brief, to the point, and grab the reader's attention.

Write headlines in six words or less for each event.

1. While walking along inspecting the mill for his boss, James Marshall discovered gold.

   _____

2. Between 75,000 and 100,000 prospectors hurried to California in 1849 to search for gold. They came by foot, by stagecoach, by horse or mule, by ship, and by wagon train.

   _____

3. President Polk confirmed the discovery of gold in a message to Congress on December 5, 1848.

   _____

4. The San Francisco newspaper stops publishing because there are too few people left to buy it. Almost everyone has left to search for gold.

   _____

5. Prices in California skyrocket. Sugar costs $2 a pound, eggs cost $3 each, coffee is $4 a pound, bread sells for $2 a loaf, and butter for $6 a pound.

   _____

6. A miner who struck it rich found $20,000 worth of gold in less than a week.

   _____

7. John Sutter asks Congress to restore title to his land in California but dies alone and poor in a Washington, D.C., hotel room before a decision is reached.

   _____

8. Mrs. Brown opened a bakery on Monday. By Friday the line of miners waiting to buy a loaf of homemade bread at $5 a loaf was almost a quarter of a mile long. Mrs. Brown says she can't bake bread fast enough to keep up with the demand.

   _____

Name: _____ Date: _____

The Klondike Gold Rush

California wasn't the only place famous for its gold rush. Another gold rush site was the Klondike region in western Yukon Territory, Canada, where the Yukon and Klondike Rivers meet.

On August 17, 1896, deposits of gold were discovered in Bonanza Creek, a branch of the Klondike River. When the news spread, another great gold rush began as people flocked north from all over the world. Conditions in the Klondike gold fields were similar to those in California during the earlier Gold Rush. Mining camps turned into boomtowns— or ghost towns. By late 1898, about 30,000 prospectors had reached the area. In 1900, miners took more than $22 million of gold from the region.

Skagway was settled between 1897 and 1898 as a port and supply point. Whitehorse became a major distribution and service center for mining settlements, and it eventually became the capital of Yukon Territory.

Another strike in the Tanana Valley of Alaska in 1902 drew miners to this site where the city of Fairbanks grew rapidly. More gold was discovered near the Chandalar and Koyukuk Rivers north of the Arctic Circle. This led to the forming of two settlements, Coldfoot and Wiseman.

Seattle, Washington, began as a boomtown during the Klondike Gold Rush and continued to grow in wealth and population when gold was discovered in Alaska. It became both a source of supplies for miners heading north and a place where many miners decided to settle after leaving the goldfields. The population increased to 80,871 by 1900 and had nearly tripled to 237,174 by 1910.

Dawson, Iditarod, McGrath, Bethel, Flat, and Ophir were other communities that developed from mining camps.

1. Select one of the cities mentioned above. Use reference sources to learn about its development as a result of either the Klondike or Alaskan Gold Rush.

_____

_____

_____

_____

_____

_____

_____

_____

Name: _____   Date: _____

Scavenger Hunt

To complete this scavenger hunt, use the Internet and other reference materials to find the answers.

1. Philip Armour made a fortune supplying meat during the California Gold Rush. He later built a huge meat packing company (Armour & Company). Where was the headquarters for Armour's meat packing business? _____

2. She began her career as a dancer in San Francisco at the age of nine. By the time she was 12, she had gained fame and fortune as "Miss Lotta, the San Francisco Favorite." What was her name?

   _____

3. This fiction writer became famous for his "local color" style of writing, which used the dialect and mannerisms of people in a particular region. One of his most popular stories was "The Luck of Roaring Camp." Who was he? _____

4. Fort Ross was originally established as a base for hunting sea otters, growing wheat and other crops, and trading with Spanish California. John Sutter bought it in 1841. What country first built Fort Ross? _____

5. James Marshall became famous for discovering gold in January 1848. What was Marshall's middle name? _____

6. When John Sutter arrived in California, he became a citizen of what country?

   _____

7. John Sutter named his estate New Helvetia. What does that mean in English?

   _____

8. The state motto of California is a Greek word that successful miners may have shouted when they discovered gold. What is the California state motto and what does it mean?

   _____

9. Lola Montez, billed as the famous "Spanish dancer," played theaters in California where she was extremely popular and earned large sums of money. However, Lola Montez wasn't her real name, and she wasn't born in Spain. Where was she born?

   _____

10. Miners who went to California by way of Panama hired natives to row them westward along the Charges River. At first, the charge was $10 per person, but as more and more miners arrived, the price rose to $50. What was the correct name of the boats used by the natives of Panama? _____

Name: _____ Date: _____

Order, Please

1. Number the events in order from 1 (first) to 10 (last). Use the time line on pages 2 and 3 for reference.

_____ A.   The first ship carrying prospectors arrived in California.

_____ B.   The Transcontinental Railroad was completed.

_____ C.   Franklin Pierce was elected President of the United States.

_____ D.   Black Bart held up his first stagecoach.

_____ E.   John Sutter emigrated to the United States.

Franklin Pierce

_____ F.   Andrew Johnson became president after Lincoln was assassinated.

_____ G.   California joined the Union.

_____ H.   The first Pony Express rider left St. Joseph, Missouri.

_____ I.   The Civil War began.

_____ J.   James Marshall discovered gold at Sutter's mill.

Andrew Johnson

2. Write two historical events that occurred **before** the events listed.

_____

_____

_____

3. Write two historical events that occurred **after** the events listed.

_____

_____

_____

Name: _____ Date: _____

World Gold Production

Gold is measured using a system based on 12 troy ounces to a pound. One troy ounce is equal to 480 grains. The amounts are listed in millions of troy ounces.

	1840-1850	1851-1875	1876-1900	1901-1925	1926-1950	1951-1975	1976-1996
Australia	0	51.7	39.7	54.5	22.9	22.4	82.9
Canada	0	2.2	4.8	21.2	85.1	87.8	72.8
South Africa	0	0	20.7	178.4	292.3	582.0	430.0
United States	5.2	58.4	51.0	93.9	66.8	40.4	109.9
USSR	7.5	22.6	29.1	24.6	73.2	134.9	133.3
All Other Countries	5.2	19.1	37.0	104.9	159.9	117.9	297.7
World Total	17.9	154.0	182.3	477.5	700.2	985.4	1126.6

1. How much more gold was produced in the United States between 1851 and 1875 than between 1840 and 1850? _____

2. What percent of the world's gold was produced in the United States between 1851 and 1875? _____

3. What percent of the world's gold was produced in the United States between 1976 and 1996? _____

4a. Which country produced the most gold between 1926 and 1950? _____

  b. What percent of the world's gold did that country produce in that time period?

  _____

5. During the entire period from 1840 to 1996, which country produced the most gold?

  _____

6. How much more gold did South Africa produce from 1926 to 1950 than the United States?

  _____

7. How much more gold was produced in Canada than in the United States between 1926 and 1975? _____

8. What was the total amount of gold produced in the United States between 1840 and 1996? _____

Name: _____ Date: _____

Search for the Gold

Look up, down, backwards, forwards, and diagonally to find and circle the 30 words hidden in the puzzle.

```
G K L G K G J Z I R I T J J T L C I S K N M M K
O G V C T Q B S R N U G G E T D J R S M T E Y B
W S L U C K Y Y B X O W H R F Y B U Z A P W V F
N K J C P Y T N A H P E L E W R T O M M N O M Z
I Y J I Q S A S H A N T Y T O W N V R X X D F U
Q M C J K Z G Y R H B N C L A I M S U A O R B J
M K P G P X V H P A I L W P B I Z B X J O Q B K
S P R O S P E C T O R S W O L O N G T O M Q S B
S R E K C O N K Y M M O T V H H R D J T G D H G
W P S W T F O Z U P C F S J D F T W J G E N C E
L U F O B W X G S A E W F O R T Y N I N E R S D
T I X K D U O N L N Z L S A J X J B H S U R K G
D R R U U L B A U N J A P N R E K C O R R T H J
D V A N D T Z U I I I Y M C S N W O T M O O B B
J K I B S X H N C N Y R A D U I M P C X S X H Z
F E X A H B W M E G X V C R Y I J X V T N T F K
D F I W D P I C Z C K N H C N C B V T J S H L S
T L N R F C X F S Z X S X I R F S O T H I Y F G
F O R T U N E K E Z Y T N Z R E W S O E W H G Z
Y F I O M E Q W D V U G E Q S N N V M Y Z T E Z
Q M D I H I Y T Y A E D T P S Z E I R F L L A L
S T U A N O G R A T Y R I C T L T Y M K D A U W
U S S D R V S S I N V H I G S O C H L T E E M L
S G U C N E J A A F S X P S N R Q M W Y G W S V
```

Adventure	Argonauts	Bart	Boomtowns	Camps
Claims	Elephant	Fever	Fortune	Forty-Niners
Ghost Towns	Gold	Long Tom	Lucky	Miner
Mining	Nugget	Panning	Picks	Prospectors
Rocker	Rush	Sail	Sand	Shantytown
Ships	Shovels	Sluice	Tommyknockers	Wealthy

1. What sport do the 49ers play? _____

2. What city are they from? _____

3. On your own paper, use the letters in CALIFORNIA to make at least 20 smaller words. Words must be three or more letters.

58

Report on the Gold Rush

Learn more about the California Gold Rush period of American history. Select one topic listed below for a three- to five-page report. Use the Internet and other reference sources and add illustrations.

Lola Montez

PEOPLE
Philip Armour
Black Bart
James Beckworth
Samuel Brannan
J. Goldsborough Bruff
Louise Clappe
Lotta Crabtree
Eliza Farnham
Bret Harte
James Marshall
Lola Montez
Sarah Pellet
Levi Strauss
John Sutter
Luzena Wilson

Samuel Brannan

EVENTS AND MINING METHODS
Chinese emigrants to the goldfields
Compromise of 1850
Coyoting method
European emigrants to the goldfields
Hydraulic mining
The Mexican War
Quartz mining
Women's rights in California

Bret Harte

PLACES
American River
California Trail
Carson Hill
Coloma
Fort Ross
Hangtown
Juan Fernandez Island
Lake of Gold
Nevada City, California
Sacramento
San Francisco
Sutter's Fort
Sutter's Mill
Yukon Territory

Sutter's Mill

Suggested Reading

The California Gold Rush (We the People) by Jean F. Blashfield

California Gold Rush: Search for Treasure by Catherine E. Chambers

California Gold Rush: A Guide to California in the 1850s by Julie Ferris

Lost in Death Valley: The True Story of Four Families in California's Gold Rush by Connie Goldsmith

Seeds of Hope: The Gold Rush Diary of Susanna Fairchild, California Territory by Kristiana Gregory

Gold Rush Fever: A Story of the Klondike, 1898 by B. Greenwood

The World Rushed In: The California Gold Rush by J.S. Holliday

The Gold Rush by Bobbie Kalman

The Gold Rush by Liza Ketchum

Answer Keys

What Is Gold? (page 5)
1. 0.000000005
2. Au
3. Au is short for *aurum,* the word for gold in Latin.
4. A mixture of two or more metals
5. A lump of precious metal
6. Density is a measurement of mass per unit volume.
7. A measurement of the purity of gold
8. A solid bar of a precious metal

The Secret Leaks Out (page 8)
2. Contemptible

The Rush Begins (page 9)
1. $10
2. $3650.00

The Forty-Niners (page 10)
1. By the time the discovery of gold was confirmed on the East coast, it was already too late in the year to head for California.
2. Jason; the Golden Fleece

Traveling by Sea (pages 13-14)
Teacher check map.

Gold Rush Homonyms (page 15)
1. carrot
2. steak
3. male
4. write/rite
5. see
6. pour
7. or/oar
8. sale
9. genes
10. routs

Too Good to Be True (page 18)
2. An armchair expert is a person who has not experienced something firsthand but pretends to be an expert on it. He or she gives advice sitting in the comfort of his or her home.

Arriving at the Gold Fields (page 19)
2. A situation that occurs when the price of goods goes up quickly
3. $36

Panning for Gold (page 20)
1. A miner stood or knelt for long hours in cold water. His hands were constantly in the cold water. In summer, it would have been very hot; in winter, often cold. The work was repetitious and boring. It was also physically difficult when continued day after day without rest.

Rocking the Cradle/True or False? (page 22)
1. T   2. F   3. F   4. F   5. T

Go for the Gold Puzzle (page 24)
1. California
2. Argonauts
3. Sluice
4. elephant
5. Tommyknockers
6. shovel
7. long tom
8. miner
9. rocker
10. rush
11. hardship
12. panning
13. ghost town
14. nugget
15. travel
Eureka!

Shantytowns and Boomtowns (page 26)
2. Only tents and shanties were erected in shantytowns. Boomtowns contained wooden homes and businesses and usually more people.

Prices: Then and Now (page 30)
List A, Then: $17   Now: Answers will vary.
List B, Then: $68   Now: Answers will vary.

Getting Rich (page 31)
1. blue jeans (denim clothing)

Gold Rush Justice (page 33)
1. A person who takes the law into his or her own hands

Black Bart (page 35)
1. Also known as
3. A mark put on clothing cleaned by a laundry
4. They could find the specific laundry and ask the owner about his or her customers.

Gold Rush Similes and Metaphors (page 37)
1. M
2. S
3. S
4. M
5. S
Check answers 11 to 15 to be certain the words *like* or *as* are not used.

What Miners Wore (page 38)
3. To cover their mouths to keep out dust, to wipe off sweat, to blow their noses, and so on

Tools of the Trade (page 39)
1. Soft leather made from deer hide.

2.

Cause and Effect (page 43)
Answers may vary. Possible answers include:
1. Thousands of gold seekers came to California.
2. The United States gained the territory of California and other territory in the southwest.
3. The stories led many others to try mining.
4. California was able to become a state in 1850.
5. Many merchants made more money than miners.
6. Vigilantes were allowed to establish order in the camps.
7. The town was created in a haphazard fashion with poorly-constructed buildings.
8. Many towns were abandoned to become ghost towns.

Women Strike It Rich (page 45)
2. A boardinghouse is a place where people can rent a room by the week or month. They provide a place to sleep, bedding, and meals.

True or False (page 47)
1. F	7. F
2. F	8. T
3. T	9. F
4. F	10. F
5. T	11. T
6. F	12. F

13. Any three: panning, rocker boxes, long toms, sluice boxes, hydraulic mining, underground mines

Fact or Opinion? (page 49)
1. F	4. F	7. O	10. F
2. O	5. F	8. O	
3. O	6. O	9. O	

Matching (page 50)
1. alloy	9. long tom
2. nugget	10. shanty
3. density	11. vigilantes
4. karat	12. prospector
5. bullion	13. pick
6. boomtown	14. kerchief
7. claim	15. inflation
8. forty-niner	16. B

There's Gold Here (page 51)
1. first	8. 50
2. pyrite	9. Goldilocks
3. plant	10. goldsmith
4. carp	11. A lazy person
5. California	12. Golden Gate Bridge
6. senior citizen	13. Ghana
(answers may vary)	14. A song that was popular
7. bird	in the past

Scavenger Hunt (page 55)
1. Chicago
2. Lotta Crabtree
3. Bret Harte
4. Russia
5. Wilson
6. Mexico
7. New Switzerland
8. Eureka!, the California state motto literally means, "I found it!"
9. Limerick, Ireland
10. bungos

Order, Please (page 56)
A.	3	F.	8
B.	9	G.	4
C.	5	H.	6
D.	10	I.	7
E.	1	J.	2

World Gold Production (page 57)
1. 53.2 million troy ounces
2. nearly 38%
3. slightly less than 10%
4a. South Africa
  b. almost 42%
5. South Africa
6. 225.5 million troy ounces
7. 65.7 million troy ounces
8. 425.6 million troy ounces

Search for the Gold (page 58)

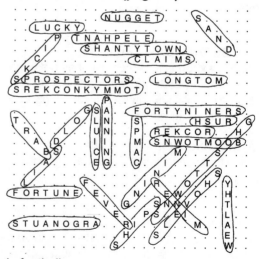

1. football
2. San Francisco
3. Some words are: acorn, afar, ail, air, arc, cairn, calf, can, canola, Carl, carol, clan, coal, coil, coin, cola, con, corn, facial, fail, fain, fair, falcon, fan, fin, final, flair, foal, focal, foil, for, frail, fun, icon, iron, lion, loaf, loin, nail, oaf, oil, orca, rail, rain, ran, roc